# *The*
# HARDEST
# JOURNEY

DOUGLAS V. STEERE

Pendle Hill Pamphlet 163

*About the Author*/Douglas Steere is Professor Emeritus of Philosophy at Haverford College and Chairman of the Friends World Committee for Consultation. His devotional and scholarly writings include *On Beginning from Within, Doors into Life, On Listening to Another,* and *On Being Present Where You Are.* He has travelled to many parts of the world on missions for the American Friends Service Committee and other Quaker organizations, and was an observer delegate of the Society of Friends at three sessions of Vatican Council II. During a recent journey with his wife, Dorothy, he took part in the colloquia between Christian and Buddhist scholars in Japan and Christian and Hindu scholars in India, under sponsorship of the Friends World Committee for Consultation.

*The Hardest Journey* was delivered as a lecture on March 5, 1968. at Stauffer Hall, Whittier College, Whittier, California, and was sponsored jointly by the college and interested Friends of California and Pacific Yearly Meetings. Subsequently it was printed as a Whittier College Bulletin in a small edition which was soon exhausted. It is here reprinted with the kind permission of Whittier College.

This West Coast lecture seeks to reach through to a common need and a common opportunity that all Friends may acknowledge and respond to. But it is hoped that the description of the cost of spiritual renewal, which is its theme, may also speak to seekers beyond the ranks of Friends.

Requests for permission to quote or to translate should be addressed to Pendle Hill Publications, Wallingford, Pa. 19086.

Library of Congress catalog number 70-76226

Printed in the United States of America by
Sowers Printing Company, Lebanon, Pennsylvania
January 1969: 4,000

# *The*

# HARDEST JOURNEY

## Douglas V. Steere

I visited Friends House in London late in January and in the course of seeing some of the Friends Service Council staff, I talked with Arthur White, who is the new Recording Clerk, or what we would term Secretary, of London Yearly Meeting. In our brief visit, he told me of the moving requests which had come to British Friends from Protestants and very especially from Roman Catholics for insights into our inward experience of silent worship and prayer and of the Quaker tradition of being sensitive to and following out concerns which may come from it.

Arthur White went on to say how humbling it was to have our inquirers look upon Quakers as seasoned veterans in the inward life when we ourselves know all too well our poverty and mediocrity in this area. But what a challenge and a goad these queries may prove if we are prepared to see them as God's nudges to us to be less unworthy custodians of our Quaker heritage.

I could and did match these appeals that he had received in Britain with similar openings that have been coming to us in the U.S.A. from Roman Catholic and Protestant brethren who beg us to share our Quaker insights into the life of prayer, of worship, of leadership of retreats, of lay ministry, as well as our experience in the non-violent resolution of conflicts. Often these people assume that our corporate and our personal lives are deeply enough centered to be ready for this kind of communication. How it searches us and makes us aware of our abysmal frailty, and yet how much of a bidding these experiences give us to pray to God that if we are not ready, we may be made ready in order that we not fail those who have been moved to ask for our witness.

## From Proclamation to Dialogue

During the spring of 1967 most of you know that the Friends World Committee under the leadership of our Japanese Quaker, Professor Yukio Irie, was host to a small religious colloquium in Japan, and another one between Hindus and Christians was held under the chairmanship of Ranjit Chetsingh. The Japanese gathering was made up of ten carefully chosen Zen Buddhist personalities, and ten Christian scholars who were ecumenically chosen, and included four Roman Catholics. A small team of five Quakers were the hosts. This group lived together at Oiso for five days and carried out a highly intimate dialogue in depth. The daily conversations were in Japanese as each person searched his own experience in order to describe his inward journey and to see how the religious tradition in which he lived might point him to a sense of social responsibility for the world in which he lived.

There was no need of academic papers. These men were the people in Japan who by experience and study could speak to each other authentically and do it without notes! There was from the outset an openness to each other that was almost breathtaking. Out of their own deep need they truly listened to each other, and with little show of personal or professional pride they asked each other, both in the public meetings and in private visits, the searching questions which I am sure they had many times put to themselves. The group had confidence enough in Quakers to accept our invitation to come, and we served as little more than friendly catalysts who helped create an atmosphere of mutual acceptance and trust. But in the course of experiencing the thrust and power in these meetings, I think Friends were given a glimpse in embryo of the new dimension of communication between Christians and men of other world religions that will mark the generation ahead.

Professor Doi speaks of this transition as the passage of Christian communication from what used to be called Proclamation to that of Dialogue in which both hearts and ears come unstopped and men begin to talk to each other again about the deepest things they know. If we believe, as Friends claim, that the Holy Spirit has long been at work in the hearts of our Zen brothers as well as at work upon our own—then in such an experience it becomes blazingly clear that the Spirit has things to say to *us* through the Zen experience and things for us to share with the Zen on the basis of our experience that each of us will ignore only at our peril.

Japan's greatest interpreter of Zen Buddhism, Professor Hisamatsu of Kyoto, had intended to be a part of this colloquium and from the very outset had been one of its most ardent sponsors. When the time came, he was too ill to attend and could only send us a message. In it he said, "All we human beings are now threatened by the crisis of the split of subjectivity, its confusion and its loss. To reverse this crisis and to create a truthful and blessed world and to realize a stable, post-modern original subjectivity—this is the universal and vital task."

This tense and twisted inward life of man, this drying up of true subjectivity, of awareness, of attention, of compassion, of inward awareness of that which is drawing at our lives from the Ground of things and this inward awareness of the unlimited liability for our fellows that has been laid upon us if we come aware of our true condition—who will stem this tide, who will reverse this crisis, who will seek to nurture a life experience that will restore in men this luminous bond, who will make himself small enough to let this life illumination surge through the eyelet of his life and reach our time? These moving words of Professor Hisamatsu's were directed to the colloquium, but they were not lost upon its hosts, the Friends. In us they raised deep questions. Do we know at first hand how true subjectivity, awareness, attention, compassion, unlimited liability for our fellows, and a return to the infinitely compassionate ground of our being can take place? And, are we ready to share what we have found?

At this same colloquium a leading Zen roshi in a personal conversation, confessed that the Zen Buddhists' deep perplexity about their responsibility for their fellows in the matter of the life of peace and of social responsibility, made them eager to turn to ask for any help that could be given them in finding their true path. Are we ready to respond to such a request?

## The Epoch of the Holy Spirit

At Vatican Council II, it was moving to see Cardinal Suenens pressing for changes in the original Schema on the Church which would indicate the Church's openness to charisms—the direct thrusts of the Holy Spirit that might come to priests or to laity or even to women! Cardinal Ruffini, a gifted scholar who almost invariably put with brilliant clarity the case for the conservative wing of the Church, countered this with an admission that it was true that there were many references to charisms in the scriptural documents recording the apostolic period of the Church, but quickly emphasized that it should be clear that the apostolic period is over, and in our present post-apostolic period, unless the Church is to be plunged into a wallow of "subjectivity," it is highly important not to encourage this kind of thing. If it did appear, it is the Church's duty to examine each charism with great care, almost implying the assumption that it is guilty until proven innocent.

Happily Cardinal Suenens' guidance and not that of Cardinal Ruffini was followed by the Council, and charisms were given a significant place in the Schema on the Church. For this great Church, with half a billion members, this may mean a whole new epoch in the acknowledgment of the freedom of the Holy Spirit to operate in other ways than simply as a support and confirmation of the decisions of the official magisterium of the Church. It may be symptomatic of the return to favor of the 13th century prophet, Joachim of Fiore, who long ago declared that in the history of that Biblical community there had been first the period of the law and the commandments, the epoch of the Father; followed by the period of the Son in which the Church and its priests played the central role; and that soon to dawn, according to Joachim of Fiore's prophecy, was the epoch of the Holy Spirit where the role of lay men and women, and of the ordinary Christian and of the Holy Spirit's communication in him and in his concerns would break through. There was to be no abandonment of either the law or the Church, but a new kindling epoch of the Holy Spirit that might affect the very fabric of society was predicted.

The witness of the Society of Friends has always been to the fact that the apostolic period of the Christian witness has never stopped; that the epoch of the Holy Spirit is upon us; and that the revelation of the power of the Spirit which the book of Acts records is in full surge. It is class-blind and color-blind and age-blind, and it comes to the plain man as well as to the genius, and given a yielding, will pour through the lives of ordinary lay men and women and through its power will release them for hallowed service in the fabric of their world.

For Friends who know no outward sacraments, this tendering

action of the Holy Spirit is the baptism; it is the communion; it is the hallower of all facets of life. It is the revealer of injustice and the dissolver of men's dikes of reservation to the costly correction of those wrongs; it is the great magnet to draw men here and now from their enmities, their violence, their wars—into the peaceable kingdom, and to soften their hard hearts to each other, restoring brotherliness and liability for each other; it is the reconciler, the enabler, the ever-present power of the inward Christ that was not only promised by the historical Jesus but that has been experienced and lived in here and now by how many millions of apostles.

The starkly elemental Quaker meetings for worship, for business, and the Quaker faith in the following of inward concerns in a trust that if they are in right ordering, way will open for their fulfillment, are built on an experience of the continual operation of this Pentecostal Spirit. Who is there in this company who has not at one time or another known the gathering power of this Spirit in our meetings and felt its power to melt them down and to lift them up, to open their hearts and to draw them into very specific acts in its service? And who here, having slipped back almost imperceptibly to shore again, has not felt his anchors being lifted, his safety ropes slipped off their dock capstans, and his boat again pushed out to sea? What a tragedy it would be if in a time when the religious scene has opened the way as at few times in its history to our witness, we should not be inwardly ready when the Great Conductor points the baton to us to come in with our note and we should sit in helpless muteness quite unable to pour out our contribution to the symphony!

## Quakers and the Hidden Life

In the field of depth psychology where almost as much new insight has come in the past half century as through the physical sciences, there is, as well, a climate of deep congeniality to the Quaker witness. Let me quote to you two rather extended but profoundly searching passages from Carl Jung with whom several Friends like Elined Kotschnig and Irene Pickard were in personal touch in the later years of his life.

The first of these passages is from Jung's earlier *Modern Man in Search of a Soul.* "Whether from an intellectual, moral or aesthetic point of view, the undercurrents of the psychic life of the West are an uninviting picture. We have built a monumental world about us, and we have slaved for it with unequalled energy. But it is so imposing because we have spent upon the outside all that is imposing in our natures—and what we find when we look within must necessarily be as it is, shabby and insufficient." The second is from his *Psychology and Alchemy:* "The divine Mediator stands outside as an image, while man remains fragmentary and untouched in the deepest parts of him. It may easily happen, therefore, that a Christian who believes in all the sacred figures is still undeveloped and unchanged in his inmost soul because he has 'all God outside' and does not experience Him in the soul. His deciding motives, his ruling interests and impulses do not spring from the sphere of Christianity, but from the unconscious and undeveloped psyche, which is as pagan and archaic as ever. Not the individual alone but the sum total of individual lives in a people proves the truth of this contention. The great events of the world as planned and executed by man do not breathe the spirit of Christianity but rather of unadorned paganism. These things originate in a psychic condition that has remained archaic and has not been even remotely touched by Christianity. The Church assumes, not altogether without reason, that the fact of having once believed leaves certain traces behind it, but of these traces nothing is to be seen in the march of events. Christian civilization has proved hollow to a terrifying degree: it is . . . veneer, but the inner man has remained untouched and therefore unchanged. His soul is out of key with his

9

external beliefs; in his soul the Christian has not kept pace with external developments. Yes, everything is to be found outside in image and in word, in Church and Bible but never inside. Inside reign the archaic gods, supreme as of old: that is to say, the inner correspondence with the outer god-image is undeveloped . . . and therefore has got stuck in heathenism. Christian education has done all that is humanly possible, but it has not been enough. Too few people have experienced the divine image as the innermost possession of their own souls. Christ only meets them from without, never from within the soul; that is why dark paganism still reigns there."

Friends who are experiencing the inward journey, the inward cleansing of the unconscious life, the inward transformation of being again and again made "tender and often contrite," and of being inwardly "joined to all the living" know all too well what Jung is talking about. They know in themselves that until they discover and are inwardly baptized into this undergirding life in which their own life is immersed, that they are still enmeshed in what George Fox called "notions." But they also know that when they yield to this "root" to which all men are grafted, it opens them to others across all barriers. They find that at this root, their fear of death fades; their fear of animals and animals' fear of them recedes, as do the terrors of the inward as of the outward night. They know how readily they can get above and beyond the "root." But they also know what it means to be brought low again and to be brought back into touch with the root.

In a world where increasingly we shall be made aware of the hidden life in us all, our Quaker witness can be deepened and enriched by the interchange of its experiences with what is authentic in the discoveries that depth psychology may produce. Are we alert and aware and ready for this interchange?

10

## The Scientific Revolution: Threat or Opportunity?

The physical sciences and the technological revolution which has come in their wake have posed a severe threat to most of the great world religions. The best minds of Islam have spent much of their energy in the last fifty years in trying to see how Islam, without losing its genius as a Divine call to men to live in the Providence of God, could accommodate itself to the Western technological revolution whose fruits the governments of its territories are determined to appropriate for their own people.

Hinduism, likewise, feels threatened by the triumph of "materialism" which it sees coming in the wake of this ever-advancing technological invasion. Buddhist scholars admit that they feel much as C. S. Lewis once described himself, "like a cavalryman in a world of tanks" with the inward dispersion and greed that seem to mark the relentless march of this Western technological sector that is moving steadily into their national economies. On the one hand, they welcome this fresh power to put a floor under the vast physical needs of their people, but on the other, they see it undermining their spiritual world-view and, whether in its 'free world' or its 'communist' setting, placing its accent overwhelmingly on 'having' rather than on 'being.'

In the Western world the Quakers have felt this conflict of science and religion less than most Christian bodies. The experiential character of their spiritual center, when it is firm, has left them very free at the periphery, and their schools and colleges, like those of the mystically-centered Brethren of the Common Life in the 15th Century, from the very outset had no fear of the new learning and the opening wide of the gates to a knowledge of the world about them. In Britain, it would seem to be more than an accident that the Society of Friends has furnished more Fellows of the Royal Society in proportion to their numbers than any other religious group.

11

There can be no denying that Quakers, too, have had among their members conservative pockets who have feared that Lyell and his geology, or Darwin and his evolution, or the Higher Criticism of the Bible, or the claims, less of science than of scientism, to have driven God out of even the gaps of the physical world—would rob them of their Lord. But there has always seemed to be a leaven at all levels of the Society who have lifted its sights above panicking at the necessary re-thinking, the re-constitution of their position which was required to confront the new face of the physical world which the scientific discoveries of the age have produced.

There is a well-known story of an old upper New York State Quaker at the time the Erie Canal was being dug who rose in meeting and expressed his strong disapproval of this bit of 'playing God' that was involved. He insisted that if God had wanted the Erie Canal dug he would have dug it himself. In due time an old Quaker woman got up quietly and quoted a text from the Old Testament, "and Jacob digged a well." This was all that she said and the matter was disposed of. A few generations later, Arthur Eddington's famous Swarthmore lecture, *Science and the Unseen World,* gave a Quaker astronomer's philosophical sketch of a complementary, rather than an antagonistic relationship, between the scientists' picture of the physical aspect of the world and the Quaker's inward experience of reality on which he has based his life.

The New England poet, Robert Frost, once noted in his homespun way that "If there is a fault to find with our time . . . it's science's failure to do all that is expected of it. We've been led to expect more of science than it can perform. Right here and now I'm telling you that there's a whole half of our lives that can't be made a science of, can't ever be made a science of. And we're going to know more about that before we get through this period. That's what it will be remembered for." (*Wisdom,* p. 19)

In Eddington's more sophisticated account of the complementary character of the scientific and the religious views of the world, there is none of Robert Frost's desire to fence off a non-scientific preserve in man, but there is in Eddington, as there is in Arnold Toynbee, an equally firm reminder that is congenial to the Quaker view that man's priorities can be badly skewed in a particular cultural age and that man in our times may have falsely exalted the omniscience of the physical sciences and neglected to attend to the other dimensions of his response to reality, dimensions such as his spiritual one, that are required to guide the findings of science if not only man's full stature is to be kept to the fore but if he is to avoid the very annihilation of his species.

There is here a potential message of the Society of Friends to our time, a message not only to our Western world but to the religions of the Middle East and Asia that could put this peculiarly balanced openness: on the one hand an openness to that which is creative in the scientific approach, and on the other a call to the inward life to yield to the tendering power of the Spirit that may alone save our world from destruction. But even if we should be able to put this message with power, and granted that many might listen, are we ready to give effective help, as we are expected to be able to do, on the inward way itself?

## The Heresy of Sheer Activism

Quakers may also be asked by their Protestant brethren in this fiercely activistic involvement in the secular world into which many of our Protestant theologians and clergy have plunged—the Jericho-Roadism of the late 60s as it may come to be known—how you keep from going over the cliff into the heresy of sheer activism. Have Quakers in their long experience with inwardly directed concerns for service found any way to

13

hold the inner and the outer together? Have they found, under the grilling pressures of situations requiring drastic social change, that they have been able to keep their own share in these things disinfected from the inevitable egotism of good works? Do we have any practical help to share about 'prayer on location' as Robert Raines calls it?

In our witness for peace have we got a word not only for the total pacifist but for the thousands of young people who are in the early stages of revulsion to killing that may not have gone beyond the specific situation of the Viet Nam War in which we are involved? And can we suggest how this beach-head of concern in a man can be nurtured until it sees further implications of what may be called for in him?

These are a few of the challenges and the almost incredible openings that beckon to Friends on the one hand, and that expose us to how much we have to do in order to be ready, on the other. Are we matched to the biddings of our time? How may we better prepare to respond to them?

Let us then turn to the inward journey that is asked of us if we are to be ready to meet these needs of our time.

### The Hardest Journey Is the Longest Journey

Dag Hammarskjold's book *Markings* is a spiritual testament to our time and it seems to me that one of his lines "The longest journey is the journey inwards" might well serve as a focus for our turning to this inward direction for the remainder of this occasion together. In another place in the book he hinted at what happened to him in the last decade of his life: "At one moment I did answer *yes* to Someone or Something— and from that hour I was certain that my existence was meaningful and that therefore my life in self-surrender had a goal." In a New Year's evening journal entry he says "For what has been—thanks! For all that shall be—yes!" But it is in that discerning line where he confesses that "the longest journey is the journey inwards," that we shall find our theme.

There is a terrible honesty in both the pulling back of the curtains upon the turning point where he answered *yes,* and the open confession to us that what follows is still the longest journey in the world. Which one of us reading this does not know what it is to say *yes?* Which of us does not know what old Dr. Sullivan meant when he asks, "Have you ever had a moment of awe and glory that has cloven your life asunder and put it together again forever different than it was before?" But what then have we done to go on in? Jan Ruysbroeck, the wonderfully gentle and attractive Flemish mystic of the 14th century says "We would not speak here of a man's first conversion nor of the first grace which was given to him when he turned. . . . But we would speak of the new gifts and new virtues from day to day and of the present coming of Christ our Bridegroom which takes place daily in our souls. . . . The Second Coming of the Bridegroom takes place every day within good men." Do we know and are we open to be tendered in our deep unconscious beings by this daily visitation? For surely it was precisely such an experience that Woolman is reporting in his *Journal* when he says that "My heart was often tender and contrite and universal love for my fellow creatures increased in me."

An English contemporary of George Fox's, the poet Thomas Traherne, puts almost the identical query in his *Centuries of Meditation* when he says, "Do you not feel yourself drawn with the expectation and desire of some Great Thing? . . . not only the contemplation of His love in the work of redemption, tho' that is wonderful, but the end for which we are redeemed: a communion with Him." Could it be that it is to this latter end of "a communion with Him" that even we ordinary people are called, and that it is the growth in awareness of the changes in ourselves that such a communion may cost that Dag Hammarskjold's word may illumine when it says that "the longest journey is the journey inwards"? For how knowingly and how honestly Dag Hammarskjold has depicted the cost of moving on in.

Most Friends have begun the journey, most know something of the initial gift, but how well do we understand and sympathize with Jesus's disciples who fell asleep again and again in the night of his passion in Gethsemane. When he needed them most, they were asleep. How close to our heart's cry is his bidding to wake up and to "come in, come in, come all the way in." How well we understand the matter of trying, as Soren Kierkegaard says, "to become a Christian . . . when one is a Christian of a sort." (*Point of View,* p. 43)

## Jean Le Clercq's Message

I have had the privilege of a friendship with a Flemish Benedictine, Jean Le Clercq, who is attached to a monastery in Luxembourg but who spends much of his time each year girdling the globe and visiting small monasteries in Africa, Asia and Latin America. His object is to encourage the monks in those small houses not to stop with their initial commitment to God, but to dare to go on in. He finds out what they long to do and then because the Roman Catholic Church cherishes tradition, and perhaps because he is the leading authority on monastic spirituality in the world today, he seeks to find for them a wonderful historical precedent and urges them to take the steps they long for.

He told me in a letter last summer that all that he was doing on this journey in Asia was to get these monks to *enjoy God* and to let the rest of the matter look after itself. I have been warmed by this word ever since I got his letter. For how better could you express the highest moments of communion, of adoration in prayer or worship than that they are just occasions to enjoy God? Paul Claudel goes as far as to say that the highest moments in prayer or worship are simply thankfulness for the existence of this great love.

The Curé d'Ars, that 19th Century French priest who drew so many needy ones from all over Europe to his simple village church confessional, tells of a peasant who used to spend half an hour each day on his knees before the altar in his church simply wrapped in prayer. Curious as to what was going on in this rough fellow, he came up to him one day and shook him and asked what was happening here anyway, to which the peasant looked up rather dazed and said, "I just look up at Him and He looks down at me." As far as I can see this peasant was going on in, and he was doing it in terms that perfectly fitted Jean Le Clercq's invitation—to enjoy God and to let the rest of the matter look after itself.

## That Which is Simple May Not Be Easy

How simple it all sounds. But that which is simple is not necessarily easy. If the whole truth is told as Hammarskjold has done, then the hardest journey that comes after the initial leading must include getting us out of our own self-absorption, our own self-imprisonment, our own self-willed determination to run our own lives according to our own plans and our own priorities and our own well-worn grooves. For until this is seriously in process, how can we talk of enjoying God?

Someone complained that a certain religious group kept talking about how religion is fun. Instead he insisted that he had found that if you meant business, it was "damned hard going," and showed little sign of easing up in the foreseeable future!

Nietzsche in his *Thus Spoke Zarathustra* has some profound things to say about friendship and among them he notes that in an authentic friend one will always find one's true enemy— that is, an enemy to that which is low in ourselves. If the enjoyment of God involves prayer and communion, and I can-

17

not see how it could do without this most direct channel that is open to a man to move along on the inward journey, then Kierkegaard may explain with an almost brutal frankness why God, like a true friend, may appear to us at moments as the enemy. For Kierkegaard can only define the very nature of prayer as "a silent surrendering of everything to God." He adds for good measure a further observation on God—the Friend-Enemy, "In thy nature and in mine and in that of every man, there is something He would do away with; with respect to all this, He repels man." (*Journals,* pp. 472, 484.)

## On Being "Still Enough to Hear God Speak"

There is a searching line in Fenelon which says, "How few there are who are still enough to hear God speak," and "How few there are,," he might perfectly well have said, "who are still enough to enjoy God." What did he mean by "still enough"? How many layers of the inward journey may lie sheathed in those words "still enough."

I once visited an old Swiss Quaker, Wolf Schwemmer, up in the high Swiss Alps in Graubunden and he took me out to see the little seat where he sat each morning for a period of time for the purpose of being still and open, of being brought low and brought back to the root—as he would have put it. I heard recently of a farmer who took one of my friends to a kind of stile over two fences that joined at right angles, where he had a seat at the top. He said that this was the place where he came to sort over and to be sorted over when the going in life got thick. This farmer would have approved of an old Virginia Quaker woman's comment that arnica was good for bruised flesh and silence or being still was good for a bruised soul. Is this kind of withdrawn stillness what Fenelon meant by being "still enough to hear God speak"? It could well be, but it is far from being the only way to listen.

## "Head of 57 Committees"

If we talk of this kind of withdrawn stillness to the person with the heat of the world on him, what will he say? The man or woman with even half an eye on professional achievement, to say nothing of those with both eyes on the main chance, is almost sure to plead that there is simply no time for this kind of semi-rustic withdrawal. Friends may have bad consciences in pleading how busy they are, but in their case they may accompany their guilty self-justification with a bill of particulars indicating how many nights a week they are spending in good works.

The late Frances Wickes, a leading New York Jungian therapist for a long generation, tells in her book *The Inner World of Choice* about a woman patient of hers who was running over with good works and who one night had a dream. "I am in a great assembly. In the center is a circular enclosure with a little gate-way. Here a man is seated writing the names of the women who enter. I see myself walking majestically through the crowd. As I reach the gate, I give my name ————— "Head of 57 Committees." (p. 60) Of course she had no time to listen, no time to enjoy. Some of us might wonder at times about the book of life and of what is being written about our own inward journey.

We have even been known to infect children with the same gallop. Frances Wickes mentions a seven year old child brought to her for sleeplessness. The child confided to her that he had to wake up at night to think, "because you can't think in the day. There isn't time." His mother had filled his day with so many opportunities.

Could it be that the pain of the neurosis which brought this first woman to the psychotherapist or that shatters many of us in our "midnight hours" is a moment of being "still enough to

19

hear God speak"? If, as C. S. Lewis indicates, "pain is God's megaphone," could it be that trapped into feeling the pain by this frantic flight from the inward journey that was so well disguised as "good works," this woman was roused by it from her form of the Gethsemane sleep, and given a chance, scars and all, to crawl back onto the real path of self-acceptance and to receive a whole new level of insight into her situation that her inward journey requires?

## "Still Enough" and the Matter of Decisions

"How few there are who are still enough to hear God speak." Is there a further dimension in this stillness that may be involved? Could "still enough" possibly mean coming nearer to the dangerous point where we might have to take certain decisions or perhaps find them taken for us by having chosen to keep company with the Friend-Enemy?

Many of us may be trying desperately to keep from making such decisions. There is a story of a Pennsylvania Dutch schoolteacher in Lancaster County who was asked by a Pennsylvania Dutch child how to pronounce the word *Aisle*. "Is it *Aisel*, teacher, oder is it *Esel?*" The teacher replied after a small interval, "Bose iss cowect." Could it possibly be that "still enough," that a real enjoyment of God, means to be open to the point where "Bose iss *not* cowect," but that one thing is to be done and another thing is to be rejected?

There is a line in the *Imitation of Christ* which says, "He in whom the Eternal Word speaks is delivered from many opinions." Could it be that to be "still enough to hear God speak" is to be still enough in the presence of the *Friend-Enemy* to settle some matters? What Quakers call a "stop in the mind" about certain courses of action may well call for decision. A little girl when asked what God said to her in her prayers that night, replied crisply, "God said, no." Hammarskjold has a line early in his *Markings* in which he says, "He who wants to keep his garden tidy does not reserve a plot for weeds."

I once stayed with a professor of philosophy in a middle western Norwegian Lutheran College. He was a very able man. Several of his books were well known and highly respected. He could almost certainly have found a post in a State University. We were talking of his heavy teaching load and of his salary which was perhaps a third of what he would have received at a State University. He finally smiled and brushed all of these things aside and said that he was quite content. He then went on to tell me that he and his wife had first gone to China in missionary work and that in making that choice, they had agreed that all they required was enough to live modestly. He went on to add that having settled that matter once, they had happily never had to reopen it again!

Matilda Wrede, the Finnish friend of prisoners who, although the daughter of the governor of Vasa, had begun her work in the Turku prison when she was only nineteen, once found that in spite of all her visits to his cell, she could not get a hardened murderer to open up his heart and talk to her. One day the door of his cell was opened and Matilde Wrede entered and was locked in quite alone and vulnerable with this prisoner who wore his heavy chains. It was late in the morning and he was as sullen as ever. She looked up at the ledge and saw there the filthy unwashed mug of weak beer that the prisoners were given each morning and that had to last them through the day. Without a quiver of fastidiousness she spoke of her thirst and asked him if she could have a drink from his mug. He looked hard at her, took the mug from the ledge, and put it in her hands. As she put her lips over it and drank from it, the prisoner broke into great sobs. That Froken Wrede had asked him to drink from his mug, that it was the first time in as many years as he could remember that he had ever been able to do anything for anyone, had overwhelmed him, and suddenly he was open.

If she had hesitated for one flash of an instant, if she had stopped to wipe the rim of the cup, if she had poured the drink into her mouth without touching with her lips the side of the mug, what might have happened? But no, she had seen the cup, had asked for the gift, and had received it from the prisoner as if it had been communion from the Lord's cup.

Is it conceivable that "still enough to hear God speak" may require decisions, lasting decisions, instant decisions, if one dares to continue to enjoy the company of the Friend-Enemy, and does it seem strange if the inward journey comes to a halt when these decisions are avoided? We may beat about the bush for a time—but dare we go on beating about the burning bush? The Zulus have a proverb "You can't ford the river without getting wet." Is a deep allergy for the dampness a possible reason why "the longest journey is the journey inwards?"

## *"Still Enough" and a Willingness to Change*

A veteran of prayer says that the conditions of the stillness, of the enjoyment of God that we have been speaking about means a willingness to change. Some of you may know that old story of how Philadelphia Yearly Meeting Friends always pray to the Lord that they may be right—for they never change! That veteran, Mrs. E. Herman, entitles a chapter of her old classic, *Creative Prayer,* "To pray is to change." Is "still enough" a willingness to have our priorities changed? Is the reason why we are so unfaithful in prayer and why we detour around the stillness, a hunch that prayer may be the place where I shall discover the next thing life is to ask of me; that to enjoy the pleasure of His company rarely takes place without feeling the lure of another step in the inward journey that is something I want, but that clearly can only be had at the cost of letting go some things that I have grown so accustomed to that I feel I cannot do without? Does Augustine's "Save me, Oh Lord, but not yet," still describe this condition?

When in his great poem John of the Cross says, "Learn that the flame of everlasting love doth burn ere it transforms"—does he refer to the stillness where the real listening alone takes place? To the young missioner who dreamed of doing thousand mile journeys, an old Rhodesian Bishop, William Gaul, suggested that it was even sweeter to God to have a man or a women who would for his sake be willing to walk the same mile a thousand times than to take the more glamorous thousand mile journey in one dramatic clump. Instead of blaming those who have opposed what I have wished to do, is it thinkable that God in the stillness might teach me that Schweitzer had the right word when he said that no one ever does anything that is out of the ordinary without many people rolling a few stones in his way, perhaps just to see if he really means it. "To be underestimated in the least is quite unbearable to us" says Francis de Sales. Is it possible that the stillness may not only thaw out our priorities but make us willing just to be tolerated by others and to help us to wear our disappointments and blockages like loose garments?

## "So Were Paul and Silas"

Does the "stillness to hear God speak" reach even to a willingness to take the consequences of our actions and very possibly to be used in some station that until now we had no notion we would ever be willing to accept? When Henry Sloane Coffin was President of Union Theological Seminary, the police called him at two o'clock one morning and told him that two of his Union Seminary students, who had been in some demonstration, were in jail. Dr. Coffin's only remark to the police before he hung up the receiver was "So were Paul and Silas." The tough and relentless love which seems to mark the Friend-Enemy in

23

his use of those who move inwards toward greater and greater 'disponibilité' is a far cry from the sentimental accounts that are often given. But the real stillness can never exclude either this dimension or the one that follows. Can it even be that an entirely helpless invalid lying in a nursing home, someone stripped of any possibility of a single overt act for others, someone who will always be a care on others, can yet do all for God and for us by the way he accepts his lot and by the kind of death, the kind of closing chapter he makes?

Is "stillness" then an almost frightening intimation that the inward journey may ultimately sweep away our reservations and may make us both tender and malleable, and that the prospect both terrifies and lures us on?

Does the want of stillness that is there even when we *do* pray, even when we *do* worship—I mean the inward distractions that clutter our prayers and cloud our worship—do even these have a message for us? When I seek to enjoy God, there tumble in on me all kinds of irrelevant thoughts and things that make my mind resemble a humming bird on holiday. What am I to do with these if they are the enemies of this stillness that will permit me to listen? I think we have some sure experience that can be of real help to those who will stop to pray and who really seek stillness. For these distracting thoughts, from which all persons suffer, do not really screen us from enjoying God if we do not try to fight against them. If we actively try to do battle with them, we are done before we begin; but if we accept them as a part of our uncollected selves and salute them and acknowledge them as present, and with them right there surrounding us, go straight on with our prayer, they no longer stand in the way.

The Jews have two theories about distracting thoughts: one is that these very thoughts know that the time of stillness is a time when a hallowing comes and they crowd in for a blessing. The other theory is even more daring. It suggests that the radiant blaze of God's presence is so consuming that we could not

24

bear Him in our present condition, so He clothes Himself in distractions in order that we can bear His presence! However you may take these ingenious Jewish theories about distractions, they are in the right mood in treating distractions as a tattered company in which I may perfectly well approach the Lord, for these distractions are a part of me. Even if I am not especially proud of them, I can accept them and come with them present, and having acknowledged them, they are no longer the focus of my attention, for I am here to enjoy God.

## "Still enough" and Growth in Tenderness

Perhaps there is another dimension of this stillness which is required if we are to hear God speak. It is a willingness to be tendered by His company. I have just read a book by an old British Quaker friend of mine, William Sewell, in which he tells of his return to West China to guide the chemistry department of a Christian college in that terrible and agonizing period of ruinous inflation and literal starvation just as Chiang Kai-Shek's regime collapsed and the Communists took over in 1948-49. He noticed the intimate tenderness of male Chinese friends who held one another's hands as they talked. One day he reached out to clasp the hand of a harassed student friend who had always held back the last increment of friendship.

I quote what he tells of this incident: "I held his hand as we talked. To me it was slightly embarrassing at first, but Min-La seemed quiet. . . . Then I saw that his eyes were filled with tears. Suddenly he burst out: 'You care; you *do* care. Your heart: it is warm.' As I continued to hold his hand, out tumbled the story." (*I Stayed in China,* p. 13) There is a classical tale of two peasants who are staying at an Inn. The first peasant says, "Tell me dost thou love me?" The 2nd says, "I love you very much indeed." The 1st, "Dost thou know what is troubling me?" The 2nd, "How can I know that?" The 1st, *Unless thou knowest what troubles me, thou canst not love me.*"

Perhaps in these two stories comes the full glimpse of the tenderness that enjoying God may involve. We may be embarrassed in the first instance, but it will mean that we enter into the only place in the world where a man is ever fully understood. And if he is to love God back there is also the need not only for him, the man, to be understood, but also the need for him to understand the love of God poured out in Jesus Christ and poured out inwardly upon us each hour of our lives and how much our failure to understand and to respond costs God. If we are to love God must we not, even as the second peasant, come to understand what the constancy of this spurned gift costs?

There is a Hasidist tale of a rabbi's son who came in drenched with tears from a game of hide-and-go-seek with some neighborhood playmates. Asked by the rabbi father what was the matter, the son told him that he had hidden and no one had bothered to seek him. The rabbi drew his son to him and said tenderly that now perhaps he could know how the dear Lord felt who had also hid himself in order to be sought and who was still waiting in vain for men to seek him! "Still enough to hear God speak" may be still enough to feel what such love costs Him.

## *The Tragedy of the Unused Life*

But there can be no depicting the hardness of the journey inward if we neglect to mention the unused life in each of us which in a very special way the stillness in God's presence, the enjoyment of God, begins to draw out of us again. For we carry within us all of the unwritten poems, the unpainted pictures, the un-made calls of loving friendship, the unwritten letters, the unheeded love of the nature around us, the unwritten books, the unreconciled hardenings toward people, the new levels of tenderness we have meant to lavish on our wives and our husbands and children, and our neighbors.

What after all is the sin against the Holy Ghost other than this unlived life, the unused light, that may die within us? Georges Bernanos, the great French Christian novelist, puts this better than anyone I know: "Won't damnation be the tardy discovery much too late, after death, of a soul absolutely unused, still carefully folded together, and spoiled the way certain precious silks are when not used? Anyone who makes use of his soul no matter how clumsily, participates in the life of the universe, becomes a part of the great rhythm and at the same time enters the great church on a level with the saint, that Communion of Saints which is the communion of all men to whom peace is promised; the holy invisible church which we know includes pagans, heretics, schismatics or even non-believers whose name God alone knows . . . the Communion of saints . . . which of us is sure of belonging to it?" (*Last Essays*, pp. 235-6) To enjoy God almost certainly is to be drawn to dig up our buried talent and to set it free to work again.

Is it because we "shun the living midnight out of which the new day comes" that we again and again become drop-outs from the inward journey? The old Hebrew patriarchs used to pile up a rock-altar and leave it behind them to mark a spot on the ground where they had experienced a break-through on the inward journey. Others coming that way who saw these rock-altars knew that something had happened there and paused for renewal. Our Indian Quaker friend, Gurdial Mallik, has composed a fresh song of thanks to God for each of the breakthroughs that have come in his own life. And he kindles his own sense of expectancy and that of others by sharing these songs. We need to remember that the hardest journey is indeed the journey inward but that it is a journey that is forever renewable, and that the greatest danger is not in stopping but in not setting out again. It is such a comfort to know that Francis of

Assisi at the very end of his life called his brothers together saying "Come brothers, let us now begin to be Christians." What an encouragement that we drop-outs are still eligible to re-enter this school once again, and to know that wood already charred by fire is not hard to set alight.

## The Bridge Between the Inward and the Outward Journey

Now there has been little in this exploration of the journey inward about the seeds of concerns that, like the unused life in us, have a way of appearing when we are still enough to hear God speak. These concerns are the bridge over which the inward journey often moves outwards. When these seeds of concerns are sown in us they are not potted plants, and much is still needed to give them what they require to grow to full stature. There is no guarantee that these concerns are infallible, although we do have certain Quaker safeguards for sorting them out; but not even the group is infallible. We may often make fools of ourselves, often fail, and often are humiliated. But I suspect that this matters very little to God if we have responded positively to these nudges. What matters is whether we fail in a learning posture and are open to further correction when life's next fork appears and we can take it and get back onto the main road again. It is a wonderful thing when the inward and the outward journey are in living connection for then we get a real sense of what it means to live in the Providence of God and to have a first-hand experience of Joachim of Fiore's "epoch of the Holy Spirit."

I think our Zen brethren have done much to teach us that you may enter on the inward journey by a thousand different gates and that no one of them dare be absolutized. You may come to the end of your tether, to the end of yourself in your vocation, and be hurtled into the inward journey; or you may because of some witness on civil rights land in jail and have a grim, boring period of incarceration; but some day you may break through to find what Katherine Mansfield meant when she said that "everything in life that is accepted undergoes a change," and that change may become blindingly clear to you.

No, there is no sacred gateway through which to pass. If I give away all my money to the poor and have a Franciscan experience of release, may not this be the way? It could be, if it brought you enduringly into a sense of unity with the vulnerable poor and made you able to answer as Meister Eckhart's beggar did when asked if it had been a good day, "I never had a poor one!" But it could affect you as it did one of my older Pendle Hill students who rued the day when she had parted with her funds. If I give up my heart and life to social work, or to occupational therapy with the mentally wounded, or to medicine, or to the ministry, or to work with migrants could this not lead me to God, to the inward journey? It could certainly do so—but it also could become a routine, loveless, over-active kind of obsession that had no more obvious Godliness in it than plumbing or truck driving, or banking—each of which might become illumined vocations. When Cardinal Leger at 65 left his critical post in Montreal to go to the Cameroons to serve African lepers—surely this was a plunge into God's intimate ranks of servants. It could be or it could be flight from a post that was of decisive importance at just this moment in history. In the outward journey there are quite as many so-called worthy roads that are what the French call a cul-de-sac—"passage sans issue" or just plain dead-ends as there are in the inward journey.

### "If Thou Knowest What Thou Doest"

There is an apocryphal story of Jesus's comment to a man seen gathering sticks on the Sabbath. "O man, if thou knowest what thou doest, blessed art thou; but if thou knowest not, thou

29

art curst." Here it is the reason for breaking the ceremonial law that is decisive, but the query holds for the whole of the outward journey. The philanthropy where "even those who wished to help, wished also to direct," or where it is urged that "we are all here on earth to help others: but what on earth the others are here for, I don't really know" is clearly a form of service that *does not know what it does,* and may well be curst, be a dead-end that opens neither the doer nor the receiver.

But when there comes from within that radical disinfection of the egotism of good works with an experience of being bound in the bundle—of all being bound in the same guilt; of knowing from within what Ecclesiastes means when it says that "for him that is joined to all the living, there is hope," then the situation is altered. When this happens we begin to glimpse what Charles Williams means by "coinherence" where we each carry and in turn are carried by others; or what Charles Peguy means when in his poem on the *Mystery of the Charity of Joan of Arc,* he writes "We must be saved together, we must come to God together. Together we must be presented before him. Together we must return to the Father's house." And when this mood of creatureliness comes, the inward and the outward journey coalesce.

If there is a single phrase that can mark both the inward and the outward journey in this epoch of the Holy Spirit in which Friends are living and to which they are called to witness, it is that we are *lent to be spent.* And the only real tragedy in it all would be that looking over the hardness of the journey, and the cost of the self-spending that is required, we should both as individual Friends and as a Society put back into our pockets the coin of destiny that has been given to us, and turn aside.

Confronted by our own and our generation's burning need, a spiritual guide of our own time may give us as Friends a final word of comfort when he declares that "not in your *skill* but in your *need* will you be blessed." May it be so!

30